CORRECTING WITHOUT CRITICIZING

The Encouraging Way To Talk To Children About Their Misbehavior

A Family Power Series Booklet

By
John F. Taylor, Ph.D.

Illustrated by
Gregory Griffith

ABOUT THE AUTHOR

John F. Taylor, Ph.D. is a family psychologist in private practice in Salem, Oregon. He is the author of such well-respected books as *Helping Your Hyperactive/Attention Deficit Child; Person To Person: Awareness Techniques;* and *Diagnostic Interviewing Of The Misbehaving Child.* He has published numerous articles in newspapers and journals. He is president of *Sun America Seminars* and frequently gives presentations to professionals throughout the United States and Canada on topics pertaining to strengthening the family.

FAMILY POWER SERIES BOOKS:
by John F. Taylor
Available from **mar·co products, inc.**

Correcting Without Criticizing
Creative Answers To Misbehavior
Encouraging The Discouraged Child
Helping Hands And Smiling Faces
Listening For Feelings
No More Sibling Rivalry

Reprinted 2002
Revised/Reprinted 1995
copyright © 1990
mar·co products, inc.

Published by
mar·co products, inc.
1443 Old York Road
Warminster, PA 18974

Library of Congress Catalog Card Number: 95-077889

ISBN: 1-884063-76-4 (Volume 3)
ISBN: 1-884063-73-X (Volume Set)

CONTENTS

INTRODUCTION

TO THE READER

The methods in this booklet apply equally to parents, teachers, counselors, youth group leaders, and any other adults charged with the supervision and care of children and teens. The child is referred to as "*your* child," even though many adults, other than the parents, will be reading this material.

The most common error made by parents is talking too much. Nagging, reminding, repeating requests, and telling children over and over to do this or not do that creates resentments in both the parent and child. Yet, ideally most misbehavior should stop after the parent confronts the child.

Criticism is a destructive act that invites revenge. Correction is a helpful art that invites cooperation. There is no such thing as constructive criticism. Founded on the untrue belief that to make children *do* better we must first make them *feel* worse, criticism usually causes more problems than the original misbehavior.

When misbehavior occurs, confronting your child is one of the most important and powerful parenting actions available to you. Ideally most discipline situations should not have to involve discipline techniques, but should be solved at the moment of confrontation. This booklet tells you how to use this powerful aspect of your relationship to increase harmony in your family. It tells you how to stay out of the nag-yell-spank cycle and how to teach your child to listen—really listen—when you talk to her or him about misbehavior. Correcting without criticizing is an important part of effective guidance for your child. It strengthens your child's love for you and improves your child's sense of emotional safety within your relationship.

HELP CHILDREN
EXPERIENCE PERSONAL POWER

One of children's most important emotional tasks is to explore personal power. A key part of successful parenting is giving children permission and guidance about how to be strong. In a sense, children need to find out what works for them, then push as far as they can toward having things become the way they would like them to be.

From the moment children first enter the world outside of their mother's womb, they have ways of letting others know when a need or urge is not being met. Infants and toddlers tend to indicate their needs directly, even if they have not yet developed language skills to ask clearly in complete sentences. If there is a major discomfort, crying occurs until it is eased, and the coos and smiles of the infant or toddler indicate the state of calmness that develops.

Part of the refreshing honesty of young children is their emotional expression. They let others know how they feel and what they need. Their natural freedom of expression can be seen as a wonderful part of their aliveness and their personhood. Children naturally enjoy the excitement and wonder of the world and of life. When they are encouraged to play freely in that world with emotional safety, they are likely to grow up with a balanced and honest pattern of expressing their emotions.

It is important to teach your child to ask honestly and directly for what he or she needs. Teaching this lesson is a lifelong gift from which your child will greatly benefit.

Teach your child how to state his or her feelings clearly and immediately. The feelings should be directed toward the person or situation that helped to trigger them. Expressed feelings are more likely to result in fulfillment of your child's emotional needs than feelings that your child hides. By teaching your child to express feelings directly and quickly toward the source person or situation, you help insure that others will listen to your child and respond in a helpful way to his or her needs.

> *Tasha is frustrated because a parent won't play with her. She might get her needs met better if she announces directly to the parent that she is frustrated and then gives a clear statement about why she is feeling that way. Such assertion on her part holds more promise of relief than suffering in silence and never discussing the issue.*

Listen to your child and give an honest answer. This teaches your child that whenever possible his or her needs can indeed be met, but only after others have a chance to find out what those needs are. Teaching children to state what they want and feel does not mean giving up adult leadership, and it does not mean letting children rule the household by turning whims into demands. It does mean listening, answering honestly, and encouraging them.

Even if the honest answer doesn't result in a change in your behavior toward your child, some good can still result. Suppose that you sense the truth in what your child is frustrated about, and you agree that your child sometimes does not receive enough attention in the form of play with you. If you explain why you are unable to play with your child, at least she or he can learn that absence of play does not mean absence of your love. Both of you can then be at peace about the matter, even though there was no increase in play.

3

Children's needs do not follow a timetable based on whenever the parents feel like attending to their needs. Children need a correct way to "interrupt." Arrange a code or standard procedure for your child. For example, your child might misbehave when bored. Set up an arrangement so that your child can use the phrase: "I'm bored" as a signal to you to assist in finding something interesting to do (see page 36 for *Suggestions For Preventing Boredom And Misbehavior*). Helping your child in this way prevents angry moments and misbehavior.

Unfortunately, many parents seem unable to get beyond this point. They consider children's concerns unimportant, insist that they are rude, demand that they not ever question what adults do, or even physically attack children. Such actions generally teach children to stop asking for what they need.

Children must experience personal power. Problems occur if parents display too much of their own power and deny their children enough of a chance to learn how to handle theirs. It is a mistake to blame or find fault with children for asserting, sensing, exercising, or feeling their own power. If you boss, are rigid and preachy, overprotect, or make too big an issue of your child's mistakes and too small an issue of successes, you force your child to search for shortcut ways to experience her or his power. This search leads to misbehavior. Power is the reason for almost every act of misbehavior. By not dominating or criticizing, you give your child the needed freedom to experience positive ways to express power. Your child will then learn to feel strong in healthy ways, such as by working toward goals and clearly stating his or her needs.

Another set of problems occur if parents don't give enough guidance in the use of personal power. Parents might display too little of their own power and allow children to have too much. If you simply agree to your child's every whim, do for your child what he or she could do without help, or become a peace-at-any-price parent, you put your child in the position of a dictator. Children have a natural desire to experience as much power as possible. This desire can lead them to become more demanding, bullying, and dominating. The more children dominate their parents, the less respect and love they sense for them. Sensing that your child has lost respect for you is frightening and upsets your relationship in many ways. Once your child attains the role of dominator, he or she will try to force you to provide guidance by making you so miserable that you will finally set some limits. An honest expression of your feelings helps your child by teaching emotional contact and directness. It also prevents you from building up anger and resentment toward your child.

What is the best way to handle your anger at something your child has just done? Having a violent tantrum, changing the subject, or keeping a phony smile and suffering in silence are not useful. Instead, use an organized approach for expressing your anger in a useful way. We *eat* apples, we *drive* cars, and what do we do with our feelings? We *announce* them! When you have unpleasant feelings about your child's actions, state them honestly, openly, and directly. Don't hide them, deny them, or try to cover them up.

Children need real human beings as models and guides. They need to learn to deal with their parents and with other adults. Part of that learning involves knowing how others feel and what they want. By being honest in expressing your needs toward your child, you are giving the gift of realness. To state feelings honestly does not mean having a tantrum, giving insults or threats, or in other ways acting hurtful. It means being emotionally honest in as calm and reasonable a manner as possible.

Some parents seem to try so hard to sugarcoat unpleasant feelings, anger, disappointment, or conflict that their children have a hard time figuring out how their parents feel or what they want. Parents who feel the need to be super nice, polite, smiling, and maple-syrup sweet at all times are actually hiding their real feelings. Parents who suddenly change the subject when conflict areas are brought up are also being emotionally dishonest.

In an effort to be nice, the sugarcoated parent might allow children to take advantage. Because of this, the parent might harbor resentments that slowly build up. One day, those resentments might come out in the form of extreme anger outbursts, causing serious damage to all the relationships in the family.

Instead of playing doormat and putting every whim of your power-driven child ahead of your own needs, set a better example. Take care of yourself, assert your needs, and refuse to allow your rights to be violated by your child or by anyone else. You cannot lift your child out of quicksand unless you are standing on solid ground. If you show your power in healthy ways, your child then has permission to also be strong and powerful. Your child can then feel safe and without fear of the scary results that occur from parents' actions that are too weak.

Change your anger into rock-solid determination. Not allowing any violation of your personal boundaries or principles is necessary for order in your family. Your anger expressed and changed in this way shows your child that you think enough of yourself to refuse to allow a violation of your personal boundaries or rights. This example allows your child to have a similar self-respect and to be equally sure about guarding her or his own personal rights against unfairness from others.

SET REALISTIC STANDARDS FOR YOUR CHILDREN

Children need set standards that are in tune with what they are able to do, in need of, and ready for. Standards set too high may lead to endless frustration for all concerned. If the standards and expectations are too far beyond their current levels of ability and understanding, children can't meet them easily enough. Discouragement and increased misbehavior are the results. If children accept the standards and try to meet them, they run the risk of concluding that they don't measure up and are stupid, worthless, or bad. If they understand these standards to be too high and therefore question their "fit," they run a risk of feeling unloved. Parents need to show that they care about their children's true wants and abilities.

If parents' standards are too low, children can meet them too easily and the door is open for two more sources of personal discouragement. First, if children accept these standards as a reflection of their true abilities, they may believe that they can accomplish any task without putting forth much effort. This view of their own abilities is certain to create problems when children face tasks at or beyond their ability level. Second, if children understand these standards to be too low, they might conclude that their parents have little faith in their abilities and the amount they are able to accomplish.

7

Matt, a second grade child, has average ability at school. Expecting Matt to learn advanced algebra will lead to one of the two negative outcomes from standards that are too high. Matt will conclude either that he is stupid in math, or that his parents are being unfair and unloving by expecting so much from him. On the other hand, expecting him to be satisfied with learning the numbers from one to ten and not going beyond that level in math will lead to one of the two negative outcomes from standards that are too low. Matt will conclude either that math is so easy that he doesn't need to pay attention in class anymore, or that his parents think he is so stupid that he won't be able to learn second grade math.

Adjust your expectations by "checking in" with your child every so often using the *Personal Private Interviews* described in this booklet on pages 15-16. Avoid too much or too little help. Instead, give help when it is needed. Stay informed about child development by reading books on parent-child relationships and similar topics. Regularly discuss your child's abilities and progress at school.

SET THE STAGE BEFORE YOU TALK TO YOUR CHILDREN

Before confronting children, parents must open up communication, establish a safe emotional climate, and start a comfortable conversation. It is important to remember that at any given time children can feel warmer and closer or colder and more emotionally distant. The goal is to provide some room for children to "back away" emotionally from their parents as the sting of their concerns is felt, yet still maintain a close and loving relationship.

Talk about your hopes for improvements in your relationship and for your child's success and happiness. Show sincere gratitude and appreciation about your child's actions and traits.

There are four keys to remember when confronting your child about the need for change in some aspect of his or her behavior.

- **Empathy:** Show that you understand.
- **Courtesy:** Treat your child with dignity.
- **Staying Brief:** Avoid nagging.
- **Timing:** Choose the right moment.

EMPATHY

One of the best ways for parents to stay emotionally close is by communicating clearly with a thoughtful and detailed display of empathy for how children feel. Showing empathy means having feelings and making statements that reflect a sincere awareness of and caring about children's feelings. The six steps for showing empathy can be represented by the first letters in the phrase: **L**ove **U**ndoes **A**ll **I**lls **C**hildren **H**ave (**LUAICH**):

L: Listening:

"Tell me more about how you feel."

Invite your child to communicate with you. Clearly express a deep interest in what your child has to say. When you give your child a "blank check" to explain completely how he or she feels, you are setting the stage for an empathic conversation.

U: Understanding:

"I understand how you feel."

This statement is the best known aspect of empathy. It is a key part of empathy and is frequently offered as a shortcut in the empathy process. However, this aspect of empathy is often done poorly because the parent merely repeats, like a parrot, what the child is saying, without showing a deep awareness of the child's feelings. Limiting your efforts by simply repeating stops far short of putting empathy to its best use in helping your child.

A: Accepting:

"I accept your feeling as real and valid from your point of view."

Despite a parent's wisdom, knowledge, and experience, children make their own decisions about what to say and how to act. Children's actions are their "best guesses" based on the total amount of information available, their maturity levels, attitudes, and their emotional condition. When confronting, you might want to help your child adjust his or her viewpoint. Remember, when your child starts a conversation with you, it is from the viewpoint of the feelings she or he is experiencing. Be sure to show your awareness of this fact.

I: Identifying:

"In the past I have felt similar to the way you now feel."

Being empathic means knowing how you would feel if you were relying on the same information and had the same emotional state and maturity level as your child. An identifying statement can reflect not only your ability to imagine how you would feel, but your actual memory of having had similar feelings. With a little bit of thought, you can use this aspect of empathy to become comforting toward your child. There are usually many aspects of your child's emotional situations to which you can relate in this way. The underlying feeling is important, not the circumstances surrounding it. If your child is frustrated because a sibling has taken something from his or her room without permission and has lost it, your memory of similar feelings does not have to be limited to having had things taken from your room. You can empathize with how it feels when things are taken away from you, when others accidentally break something important to you, when others come uninvited into your home or room, or when others let you down.

C: Caring:

"I care about you and wish you happiness, so I don't want you to be having this painful emotional experience."

No message of empathy is complete without a clear indication of "I care." The very core of empathy is caring. This is best shown by your wish that your child experience pleasant feelings and positive events in life. In addition to showing caring for your child, this aspect of empathy also reflects, "I wish you well."

H: Helping:

"How can I help you so you'll feel better?"

The natural next step after understanding and identifying with your child's unpleasant feelings is to do with her or him what you would want to do with your own similar feelings—find a way to make things better. Your desire to be of help is a powerful aspect of true empathy.

COURTESY

Basic personal courtesy is very important when confronting children. Here are a few of the most often made errors. Be sure that you keep these ideas in mind as you prepare to confront your child. Stay focused on what your child is saying, and avoid thinking about other things while conversing.

Never start by accusing your child of doing something bad or wrong. "I have a bone to pick with you" is a terrible first line! The first words of your confrontation, and all further statements as well, should be friendly, not hostile. Never interrupt your child when he or she is talking about the incident. To interrupt is to give a very big insult, and an argument may start.

Convey trust in your child. Convey confidence in your child's judgment and abilities.

Speak in a tone of voice that you would use if you were conversing with someone ten years older. Don't talk to children or adolescents as if they were much younger. For example, your voice tone while you talk with an eleven-year-old child should be about the same as it would be if you were talking with a twenty-one-year-old.

STAYING BRIEF

State all of your messages with few words, so that everything you say is meaningful. Words used to direct children are like tires. The more times a tire goes around, the more tread it loses and the less efficient it becomes at starting, stopping, and steering. In the same way, the more words you use to start, stop, and steer your child's behavior, the less efficient those words become. Your child will gradually become too used to the words, so that you might feel the need to raise your voice or combine words with threats to get the message across. Good confronting doesn't involve threats and raised voices. It avoids both.

TIMING

Timing is important for your child's sake as well as your own. Be sensitive about where and when to confront. Information that might be embarrassing or that might lower your child's image among friends, relatives, or family members should be discussed in private. Avoid giving negative messages to your child when he or she is already upset, angry, or saddened.

When you are under great stress, tired, feeling overwhelmed, angry, or emotionally drained, do everything you can to get calm before confronting your child. Find a way to reduce your anger so that you can perform your confrontation well. Consider going into another room, counting to ten, getting a glass of water, writing down your concerns, or taking a shower or bath. There is no need to confront your child at the moment of misbehavior. A few moments to calm down and gather your thoughts will result in a better confrontation and an improved relationship with your child.

When you are exhausted and emotionally drained, simply state that you need to be alone for the next half hour and cannot answer any more questions or talk to anyone during that time. Then, go to a protected place—your bedroom or the bathroom—to get the privacy and stress relief that you need.

ROUTINE STRUCTURED TIMES TO GIVE CORRECTIVE FEEDBACK

It is very important to talk with children about the various issues of family living at times other than when an upsetting incident has occurred. Two types of scheduled discussions are very useful for giving constructive feedback to children about ongoing behavior: Personal Private Interviews (PPI's) and the Family Council. A third procedure, Therapeutic Affection, is also useful as a way to prepare children for confrontation about misbehavior.

PERSONAL PRIVATE INTERVIEWS

Have regular Personal Private Interviews with each of your children. These meetings should occur in a private place such as your child's bedroom. Your role at the meeting is similar to that of a news reporter. You want to discuss how your child is doing in the major areas of day-to-day living. Review school needs, social life, material needs (clothing, personal grooming items, etc.), medical needs, and your child's daily routines including chores.

To prepare for upcoming PPI's, parents should have a Concerns Notebook in which to note events and issues for discussion. Children should have their own Concerns Notebook also, in which they write down gripes, issues, questions, conflicts, and needs for discussion at the upcoming PPI.

Parents who have used this method are usually quite pleased at how simple and effective it is at keeping all of their children's problems small and solvable. Issues never go unnoticed, but instead are dealt with openly and directly in a safe emotional climate on a once-a-week or once-every-two-weeks schedule.

To learn to assert honestly for his or her needs, your child must experience that assertions are safe as well as productive. You can make them safe by providing the emotional climate outlined in this booklet. You can make them productive by responding to your child's concerns given in the PPI's. There is no need to answer your child's requests during the meeting unless it is convenient to do so. Simply arrange a time by which you will have a response ready. Allow yourself some time to gather information; discuss the issues with those involved; obtain any needed money for purchases; and make all other preparations for giving a helpful, empathic, and effective answer to your child's requests and concerns. At least partially, try to fulfill what your child has asked for, so your child will want to continue having the PPI's.

Another advantage of this method is that it gives you a way to check on the various changes you have requested in your child's behavior. Your child will quickly learn that he or she will have to face you at the next PPI to explain the results of the behavior changes you have requested. Limit such requests to one per PPI so that most of the PPI consists of your checking on your child's needs through the interview process.

FAMILY COUNCIL

Children need a safe and effective arena in which to discuss rules, routines, chores, and concerns within the family. Regular weekly meetings are very helpful. These meetings help children feel loved because parents are listening to their needs.

In contrast to PPI's, Family Council meetings include the entire family as a group. Hearing the concerns of others given calmly in the spirit of open communication helps children learn how to improve their relationships with each other.

The basic idea is simple—regular meetings of the entire family to discuss issues, make plans, share concerns, solve problems, agree on solutions, and show their love for one another. It allows children a voice in the affairs of the family while at the same time gives parents a safe place for providing leadership.

In addition to a review of schedules and activities of the members of the family, the Family Council involves a discussion of chores and routines. Any family member can make suggestions for changing the family's routines. In most families, many daily and weekly routines center on such areas as food, clothing, house cleaning, lawn care, planning for outings, pet care, allowances, car care, and room cleaning.

Concerns and negotiations are important parts of the Family Council. Discuss difficulties or conflicts experienced by any family member. Develop solutions and try to reach an agreement on which solution to try. Try one solution at a time until you find one that works best. Try each solution for several days and discuss the issue at additional Family Council meetings until it is solved. This open and accepting climate encourages the discussion of all important issues facing your family.

During the Family Council, one person reviews and records the agreements and plans made. This record helps prevent later misunderstandings among family members. It can be written or tape-recorded. A good way to close a Family Council meeting is with games, singing, story telling, refreshments, or a similar experience. With a little bit of advance planning, the Family Council can become the basis of regular togetherness for your family.

An important aspect of parent leadership during a Family Council meeting is guarding children's rights to express their concerns and opinions. As they attend more Family Council meetings, children tend to put more thought into their opinions, and their suggestions become more useful.

A helpful procedure for Family Council meetings is to have family members write down topics on slips of paper and put them into a "discussion box." A problem is anything for which a family member wants helpful action. Concerns can include frustrations that happen to family members—called "bugs." Things that happen in the family that are confusing to the children and about which they want more information are called "puzzles." The children write down problems, bugs, and puzzles on separate slips of paper. Each week, the family discusses the items from the box. Younger children can have someone write down for them a few key words as a problem, bug, or puzzle.

THERAPEUTIC AFFECTION

Sometimes, children misbehave because they are out-of-sorts, tired, bored, frustrated, or in other ways reaching the end of their rope. In such circumstances, Therapeutic Affection is very useful for breaking up the situation and paving the way for confronting children. Parents who use it are often surprised at how powerful it is, and they continue to use it year after year because it is so helpful. It involves four parts, symbolized by **TEAM**.

T stands for **Touch.**

Start by giving appropriate touches, the more the better. Place a small child on your lap, embrace, and start a slow, gentle rocking motion. If lap-sitting is not suitable, sit next to and lean against your child, with your arm around your child's shoulder. If that type or amount of skin contact would not be acceptable for any reason, gently rub the shoulder or arm of your child while sitting next to him or her.

E stands for **Empathy.**

Your child expects negative statements from you—scolding, nagging, and similar kinds of talk. During Therapeutic Affection you give no such messages. Instead, give nothing but empathy. Your first statements should show your awareness and concern about your child's feelings:

> *"You're angry at Josh right now, aren't you?"*
> *"It looks as if you're getting pretty tired now."*

If you are unsure about just what your child is feeling, use the blanket empathy statement:

> *"This is a hard time for you, isn't it!"*

Skipping the empathy phase of confrontation creates many problems. Your child may become angry at you and show a desire to hurt you by not doing what you request. Do not rush empathy. Allow it to run its course; wait for indications that your child is ready to move on, at least two minutes.

A stands for **Affirmation.**

Indicate that you love your child and want your child to feel better. For example:

> *"I don't want you to feel so angry at your brother, because then neither of you can be happy when you are together."*

Statements about your love for your child are useful:

> *"I love you and I want you to be happy."*
> *"I'm sorry that you feel so bothered right now."*

Just as tea needs to sit for a while to blend and come to its full flavor, so your "tea" of Therapeutic Affection needs to "brew" and continue for a brief while also. Allow your conversation to switch back and forth between empathy and affirmation while you continue to hold, touch, or gently rock your child.

M stands for **Moving.**

Don't simply send your child back into the situation where the misbehavior occurred. Without rushing to end the "tea" phase, respond to any squirming, looking around the room, or other indication that your child is ready to resume normal activities. Invite your child to join you in some pleasant, quiet activity such as helping you perform a minor chore, working with arts and crafts, making something in the kitchen, or doing some other activity away from the scene of the trouble.

At a later time, discuss the misbehavior as you would any other incident, at the next PPI or at bedtime that night. The Therapeutic Affection method indeed makes you and your child an effective TEAM for solving moments of misbehavior.

SAY "I CARE" BY
CONFRONTING YOUR CHILD

Confrontation should teach things to parents as well as to children. Children should learn about better behavior choices, and parents should learn more about children's needs. Parents can then adjust their expectations and actions to prevent future misbehavior.

FIVE STEPS FOR BETTER BEHAVIOR MANAGEMENT

Effective confronting of children about misbehavior involves five basic steps, **I CARE**:

I: Interrupt:

Be willing to interrupt the ongoing process and break up the scene. For example, separate your children and send them off in different directions. Intervene so that the negative behavior comes to a stop and your children must deal with you.

There may be times when you would not want to interrupt ongoing misbehavior. Often, the best form of disciplinary approach is to avoid overinvolvement and stay out of a situation. However, if you are purposely avoiding getting involved as part of your discipline approach, you will not be able to confront your children successfully. If you wish to confront them, you must make your presence known.

Use the Huddle System. Call your child aside and confront him or her about the misbehavior that is starting to occur. Be calm and organized, and follow the guidelines in this booklet. Agree ahead of time that either of you can call for a huddle whenever something goes wrong in your relationship or in the actions one of you is taking.

C: Cool Off:

Both of you need to cool off. Consider sending your child to a cooling-off place such as the bedroom for a few moments prior to the confrontation with you. Therapeutic Affection is usually very effective at helping your child cool off emotionally to prepare for a discussion with you about the misbehavior. It is more important, however, that *you* cool off than your child cool off.

A: Affirm:

Express faith in your child's judgment and ability to understand what you are saying. Assume that your child is willing to cooperate. Include honest appreciation for the helpful things your child does. Point out that your child works hard, has a pleasant attitude, tries hard, or is pleasant to be with at certain times or circumstances. Be sincere and choose traits that you truly appreciate.

R: Redirect:

After breaking up the misbehavior, steer your child in a new direction. One useful way to redirect your child is to have your child reenter the situation to undo or redo what has just happened.

- *Undoing* means cleaning up the mess and repairing the situation after the misbehavior has occurred. For example, when a toy is broken, the child is expected to apologize and replace it.

- *Redoing* means starting a situation over in a new and improved way. For example, to redo an unpleasant moment, the child suggests a friendly way to play.

Consider having a Fun Idea List available, so that your child can get instant ideas about some interesting things to do when boredom sets in. *(See page 36 for a listing of fun things your child can do to prevent boredom-based misbehavior. Make your own Fun Idea List.)*

E: Educate:

Figure out what happens in the few moments leading up to your child's misbehavior. These events provide clues to hidden purposes in misbehaving. Find better methods for your child to satisfy the needs that seem to be met by the misbehavior.*

A very useful method is to give feedback based on the labeling of moments of misbehavior. Arrange to tell your child a special code word for the misbehavior you are helping to make your child more aware of. Say:

"This is one of those times."

Then, say the code word to your child whenever you notice the misbehavior. The code word system is much better than endless nagging and reminding, which of course frustrates both you and your child and does more harm than good to your relationship. For example:

"From now on, Tyrone, I want to help you realize when it is that you are simply playing too rough with Kesha. Whenever I notice it, I will say the secret code word 'Red Flag.' This means that I'm pretending to wave a red flag at you to alert you to the fact that this is one of those times when you are playing too rough. When you hear the code word, stop playing in whatever way you are, and start playing in a different, more gentle way."

---

* For detailed guides to using misbehavior as clues to any child's needs, see *Understanding Misbehavior,* available from **mar•co products, inc.,** 1443 Old York Road, Warminster, PA 18974.

Help your child think about the effects of behavior and consider how to make improvements for the future by asking:

"What can we learn from this?"

Also, talking about "next time" in a positive way is very encouraging to your child:

"What can you change so next time will be better?"

In general, parents who are encouraging refer to the helpful aspects of the future, and parents who are discouraging keep bringing up negatives about the past.

FIVE STEPS FOR EFFECTIVE CONFRONTATION

The way to instruct children about how to improve for "next time" is to provide these five steps:

Step 1: Describe The Situation

Tell your child how the misbehavior directly affects others in a negative way. Help your child understand the misbehavior's direct impact on others.

"Every time you take the ball from Lisa, she thinks you are mad at her, and she starts to feel sad and confused."

Call the misbehavior a mistake. It is an error.

"I think you are making an important mistake about Sherry, and I'd like to talk with you about it."

Start by describing clearly and specifically what was actually seen. Objective reporting of countable, outward actions is more helpful than jumping to conclusions, making wrong guesses about your child's motives, or labeling your child.

24

Pointing out how many times you have heard your child's improper statements to a sibling is much more helpful than calling your child a loudmouth or a pest.

Step 2: State Your Feelings

Don't be afraid to tell your child how you feel about what is happening, at the first moment that you are ready to do so. Not letting your child know how you are affected by the misbehavior robs your child of important tools for learning how to improve relationships with others. Your sharing of feelings is a form of contact that allows your child to sense that you are genuinely trying to "connect" emotionally. This honest stating of feelings helps family harmony and sets a useful example.

Current feelings and actions are better to talk about than past history or predictions for the future. State that you are angry at your child *right now:*

> *"Zach, I'm angry right now because of what you did."*

State how you feel. Be honest:

> *"If you are doing this, I feel somewhat disappointed about my efforts to teach you how I wanted you to act."*

Step 3: Ask For Changes

Tell your child once, very clearly, completely, firmly, and calmly, what you wish him or her to start or stop doing.

Express your want in the form of a hope or wish:

> *"I hope you will want to start doing your homework before seven o'clock from now on."*

Suggest possibilities for your child to consider and state your reasons beyond "just because," or "because I'm your parent."

Be specific and clear. If you are too indirect or vague when expressing what you want from your child, you create more problems. One possible result is that your child might start to develop guilt feelings about not being able to satisfy you. Your child would sense only that you are somehow unaccepting and dissatisfied. Your child might also start to resent or even hate you for having so much power and for giving what amounts to rejection messages.

By receiving a clear statement of how you feel and what you want, your child can better feel the joy of helping and of responding to your emotional needs.

Step 4: Offer To Support Your Child's Changes

Treat the misbehavior as a small mistake that can be corrected easily and quickly. Suggest corrections that can be made. Be encouraging and indicate that the whole matter can be cleared up quickly.

Emphasize the practical need for the corrections requested. Your child needs to become aware of the importance of not making the error. Try to show how much others depend on your child. Show the real results of the error, calmly and without threats or long-term predictions of doom.

Show your child that privileges will be lost if abused and granted if handled responsibly.

Step 5: Check On Understanding And Acceptance

The purpose is to win an agreement, not an argument. Conflicts are easier to solve in a climate of trust and mutual respect. Tact helps.

Treat the conflict as a problem that needs to be solved jointly. Focus on finding a solution that allows everyone's needs to be met without frustration. Mutual respect leading to mutual satisfaction goes a long way toward stopping misunderstandings.

Let children save face by defending and explaining their actions. Get your child's view of the problem, feelings, and ideas about possible solutions. After listening carefully, respectfully, and calmly to your child's point of view, repeat it in your own words, even if you don't agree with all parts of it. Putting your child's explanation into your own words shows understanding and concern. Such empathy can help your child understand your point of view later on.

Rather than proving how wrong your child is, help your child become right. Put your efforts into changing your child's position rather than simply judging it as off base. Do things with your child to explore the issue as a helpful ally. Offer to learn about the issues together by reading a book or attending a public lecture on the topic, then discussing it.

State your position calmly and give reasons for it. State that you want your child to understand your point of view. If you have evidences, express confidence that your child does indeed understand.

If your child is starting a power struggle by yes-butting your ideas and rejecting all suggested alternatives, say:

"I'm not going to debate or argue with you. You might be right, but I still want you to do it this way because..."

If necessary, ask for an "experimental solution" and talk about results later, perhaps at the next Personal Private Interview or Family Council.

Parents need to guide children to consider the impact of their misbehavior on themselves and others. Invite them to think of some possible solutions. This process is part of teaching children how to make better decisions. The six steps in decision making that help children learn to make wiser choices about their behavior are:

- Name the problem
- Gather data
- Identify the choices
- Consider the consequences of the choices
- Decide what to do
- Evaluate later on

The six steps of decision making apply to any form of repeated misbehavior. The misbehavior reflected in the following table is breaking the rules of a diet by eating forbidden food while the parents were away from home.

HOW TO TEACH DECISION-MAKING SKILLS*

DECISION-MAKING STEPS	INEFFECTIVE METHOD	EFFECTIVE METHOD
NAME THE PROBLEM	Name-calling, accusing: *"You're not paying attention to your diet anymore." "You must not care about your health."*	Specific, countable: *"Three times this week you have eaten something off-limits."*
GATHER DATA	Assume you already know all there is to know: *"I know what you were thinking, and I don't want any of your excuses."*	Find out the facts; search out the child's logic and feelings: *"Have there been more instances that I'm not aware of?" "Do you agree that all three were off-limits?"*
IDENTIFY THE CHOICES	Preach, give no choices; child listens and you do all the talking: *"From now on, I'm never letting you stay home alone, and you'll never be allowed to have any..."*	Encourage child to think of solutions; give choices: *"What can we change so that you will be less tempted next time?" "What other things could you do instead of eating at those temptation times?"*
CONSIDER THE CONSEQUENCES OF THE CHOICES	Assume that your decision is the best one; demand that the child obey: *"If you ever do this again, you're going to get it!" "There's no point in trying to talk to me about it."*	Use "If...then" logic: *"If I remove that type of food from the kitchen, then our family will need to find a substitute."* Explore pros and cons of each choice: *"What do you think about each of these plans?"*
DECIDE WHAT TO DO	Decide instantly while angry; offer no decision: *"You're grounded for a week; the topic is closed."*	Give each child credit for thinking of possible solutions; compromise; base decisions on needs of entire family: *"Let's reach the best solution that meets your needs and protects you—and protects us—from any more of these types of mistakes. You write down our decisions so you'll be sure to know them in the future. We'll discuss them at the next family council."*
EVALUATE LATER ON	No communication with child about the issue until another diet break occurs; no arrangement to check on results of planned changes.	Discuss results at a planned and scheduled time, usually several days after the incident; allow changes in arrangements. At the next Family Council or PPI: *"Do you think that our plan is working?" "Is there anything about it that you think should be changed?"*

*From: *Why Can't I Eat That! Helping Kids Obey Medical Diets*; John Taylor & R. Sharon Latta, R & E Publishers, San Jose, CA, 1993.

DESTRUCTIVE ROLES TO AVOID

Here are four roles to avoid when confronting children. Each of these roles brings its own set of dangers.

COMMANDER-IN-CHIEF

The Commander-In-Chief needs to control everything and everybody by giving a constant stream of orders and demands. The most frequent statements are "You must," "You will," and "You have to." Children are told to stop showing negative behavior, and there are many threats and warnings of "You had better, or else."

The key to avoiding the Commander-In-Chief role is to focus on controlling yourself, not your child. When in self-control, you can listen and take time for your child's concerns. *When you are not in self-control, you risk trying to overcontrol your child.*

Avoid feeling power by how much bigger you are and how small your child is. Decide to avoid force or power as your main method of affecting your child's behavior. Stop trying to apply pressure; invite shared decision making instead.

Telling your child about the unacceptable behavior is often enough. Simply providing a direct statement of the impact of the actions on others may be sufficient.

"When you did that, it made Bill sad because..."

CRITICAL JUDGE

The Critical Judge is too quick to decide about things. Children's actions are seen as too negative, and they are blamed too quickly. Name-calling is also done by Critical Judges:

"You are a bad boy."
"You are not thinking straight."
"You are disappointing me again."

Critical Judges are out to prove themselves right and children wrong. Children are found guilty without a fair hearing of their side of things. There is an attempt to humble them by put-downs. The Critical Judge believes that it is proper and effective to point out their flaws in order to get the children to correct them.

Accusing your child of being a bad person does nothing helpful. Your child will become defensive and guarded if critically judged by you. Your child wants you to hear her or his thoughts and ideas, not judgments of what is good, bad, right, or wrong about her or his opinions. Accusing your child of having an undesirable motive, such as wanting to show off, does little other than harm communication between the two of you. It ruins any chance for emotional safety.

Avoid saying how right you are and how wrong your child is. Avoid jumping to conclusions. If you have never really "caught" your child at the misbehavior in question, be very careful about accusing him or her or relying on too little evidence.

Remember that the mistake—the misbehavior—is being corrected. Treat your child like a VIP who is always worth listening to. Avoid the following booby traps:

Threats:

"You'll be sorry!"
"I'll send you to a foster home and you'll never come back."

Long term predictions:

"You'll end up in prison some day."

History lessons are not helpful. Don't make extreme claims:

*"You **always** do things like this!"*
*"You **never** remember to do that the way I told you to."*

Such statements are easily proved incorrect.

Never say that you think your child can't do anything right. Avoid name-calling. Any criticisms of his or her attitude, abilities, energy, honesty, cooperativeness, or personality will cause harm.

This table contrasts encouraging with discouraging messages that the Critical Judge sends when confronting a child about misbehavior. The misbehavior in this table is eating food that is not allowed in the child's diet.

CRITICAL JUDGE	ENCOURAGING PARENT
" Give up. You obviously can't resist the temptation to go off your diet anyway."	" Don't let yourself be discouraged by this one mistake."
" You've never been good at staying on this diet, and this proves it."	" You've made a few mistakes about food choices, but you're making fewer as time goes on."
" You're still goofing the diet up. Can't you ever get it straight?"	" You are making fewer of these types of mistakes."
" You're not doing as well as Tammi at staying on your diet. Don't you want to do as well as she does?"	" Never mind how Tammi is doing. Compare yourself with your own progress—you're making fewer of these types of food mistakes, and that's what's important."
" You'll never be able to stay on any diet."	" You will make fewer of these types of mistakes in food choices as you get more practice with the diet."
" Next time we're not home, I suppose you'll sneak into the kitchen and take the wrong food again."	" Maybe next time can be better, because after our little talk, I will keep more of the right food for you in the cupboard."
" There is no excuse for eating the wrong kinds of food."	" Let's see what's causing you trouble in these situations."
"This going off the diet is terrible, horrible."	" The world won't come to an end because of this, but we'd better change something so it doesn't keep happening."
" This break in your diet means that all of your effort and my effort so far is nothing but a big waste of time."	" Let's not waste this experience. What can we learn from it so that next time will be better?"

KNOW-IT-ALL

The Know-It-All parent questions, probes, and cross-examines:

"Why did you do that?"
"What did you do that for?"

There is often a display of knowledge and a need to lecture to children. The key for avoiding the Know-It-All role is to decide that you will use shared data. An ancient fable illustrates this point.

> Once there were four blind men standing with an elephant, trying to decide what an elephant is. As each man felt a different part of the beast, he claimed to have found out the true nature of an elephant. One said that an elephant is like a fire hose; another, that an elephant is like a giant leaf; the third, that an elephant is like a wall; and the fourth, that an elephant is like a rope. The one process needed so that they could be accurate about the elephant would have been to add all of their information together. Instead, the ancient tale states, they argued forever among each other about what an elephant is.

These blind men were Know-It-Alls. Each claimed that his own information was all that was needed for coming to a full understanding. For your part, vow that you will listen to your children's points of view and explanations without jumping to conclusions. Gather the data well so you can be most helpful to your children.

COMEDIAN

The Comedian kids, teases, and uses sarcasm:

"Why don't you just burn the house down!"
"Aren't you well behaved!"

To avoid the Comedian role, remind yourself that humor is dangerous in close relationships. Rarely can it be successfully used in confrontation. It is better to set humor aside when talking seriously with loved ones. Save humor for lighthearted moments that are not so important for your relationship with your child.

EFFECTIVE CONFRONTING

Some of the key principles of *Correcting Without Criticizing* are given in this table. Review often to remind yourself about how to be encouraging as you confront your children about misbehavior.

EFFECTIVE CONFRONTING (Correcting)	INEFFECTIVE CONFRONTING (Criticizing)
⇨ Child is asked for opinion	⇨ Child is told what to think
⇨ Two-way communication	⇨ One-way communication, parent talks, child listens
⇨ Child has choices, is able to consider options	⇨ Child has no choice; is told what to do
⇨ Child's logic is discovered	⇨ Child's logic is not discovered
⇨ Ask leading questions	⇨ Preach
⇨ Respect child	⇨ Accuse
⇨ Problem solve	⇨ Demand obedience
⇨ Promotes harmony	⇨ Destroys harmony
⇨ Request that child consider adult's point of view	⇨ Demand that child accept adult's point of view
⇨ Acceptance of child's point of view as a valid option	⇨ Rejection of child's point of view as not valid
⇨ Resolves underlying issues leading to the misbehavior	⇨ Basic issue and child's needs are not resolved
⇨ Parent does not give repeated messages	⇨ Parent is wordy, preachy
⇨ Parent models values being taught—courtesy, kindness	⇨ Parent models being demanding and bossy

SUGGESTIONS FOR PREVENTING BOREDOM AND MISBEHAVIOR*

These suggestions were provided by many parents as being effective in helping easily bored children channel their energy. Use this list as a starting point and change it to fit your family's specific needs. Along with numerous other strategies for preventing boredom and misbehavior, the Fun Idea List and Fun Idea Drawer are discussed in *Helping Your Hyperactive/Attention Deficit Child.*

OUTDOOR OR GOOD WEATHER PLAY REQUIRING OTHER CHILDREN

■ HAVE A POPCORN AND FRUIT DRINK STAND ■ CAMP IN THE BACK YARD IN SLEEPING BAGS OR TENTS ■ GO FOR A WALK OR HIKE ■ PARTICIPATE IN A VIGOROUS ACTIVITY LIKE SWIMMING, RUNNING GAMES, OR BALL GAMES ■ DO WATER PLAY WITH A HOSE AND PLASTIC SLIDE CLOTH ■ HAVE A WATER FIGHT WITH SQUIRT GUNS AND CUPS, USING BUCKETS OF WATER AS THE SOURCE OF "AMMUNITION" ■ DO A SUPERVISED LONG DISTANCE BIKE HIKE AS A GROUP

INDOOR OR BAD WEATHER PLAY REQUIRING OTHER CHILDREN

■ PLAY JACKS ■ PLAY CARD GAMES ■ MAKE A TENT WITH A SHEET AND A CARD TABLE ■ TELEPHONE A FRIEND ■ GATHER SHOES TOGETHER FROM AROUND THE HOUSE AND PLAY SHOE STORE ■ USING A COMB, CUP WITH WATER, AND TOWEL, PLAY HAIRDRESSER OR BARBER ■ PUT THINGS IN A MYSTERY SACK AND GIVE CLUES ABOUT WHAT IS IN THE SACK, ALLOWING THE OTHER CHILD TO REACH INTO THE SACK AND FEEL THE OBJECT AS THE LAST CLUE ■ MAKE UP A PRETEND RADIO OR TELEVISION INTERVIEW AND TALK INTO THE RECORDER

OUTDOOR OR GOOD WEATHER SOLITARY PLAY

■ WATCH THE STARS THROUGH A TELESCOPE ■ LOOK THROUGH THE BINOCULARS ■ WORK ON GARDENING ■ HUG A TREE ■ LINE UP SODA CANS AND THROW PEBBLES AT THEM ■ FEED PETS ■ PRACTICE JUMP ROPE STUNTS ■ DRAW PICTURES OF YOUR YARD TO SHOW THE SEASONS OF THE YEAR ■ WATER SOME FLOWERS WITH A SPRINKLING CAN ■ MAKE A COLLECTION OF LEAVES FROM THE YARD ■ SWAT FLIES ■ FEED SPIDERS ■ VOLUNTEER TO SWEEP A NEIGHBOR'S SIDEWALK WITHOUT PAY ■ DRAW A PORTRAIT OF A HOUSE, TREE, OR OTHER OUTDOOR SCENE ON AN ART PAD ■ PLAY ON A CLIMBING STRUCTURE OR SWING SET ■ PLAY IN A SANDBOX ■ ROLLER SKATE ■ RIDE A BIKE ■ BUILD SOMETHING FOR BACK YARD (BIRD HOUSE, BIRD FEEDER) ■ USE A SKATEBOARD ■ GO JOGGING ■ GO SWIMMING ■ GO FISHING ■ ICE SKATE ■ GO HORSEBACK RIDING ■ TRAIN AND GROOM PETS ■ EARN MONEY BY WASHING CARS OR MOWING LAWNS ■ WRITE OR DRAW ON THE SIDEWALK WITH CHALK

---

* From *Helping Your Hyperactive/Attention Deficit Child,* available from **mar·co products, inc.,** 1443 Old York Road, Warminster, PA 18974.